INSPIRING TRUE STORIES BOOK FOR 6 YEAR OLD GIRLS!

I am 6 and Amazing

Inspiring True Stories of Courage, Self-Love, and self-Confidence

Paula Collins.

Contents

Introduction

Hello! Do you realize how amazing you are?

You are exceptional. You are completely unique. Always remember that! You are the only you there is in the entire world, and that's out of billions of people!

The world has many big and small hurdles in store for you. Sometimes you might think that you can't make it. You might get very scared or doubt yourself. However, I want to tell you a secret. Everybody feels like this from time to time! Even adults.

In this Inspiring Stories book, you will meet other amazing girls. These girls overcome their fears, show great inner strength, and reveal their bravery.

Of course, you can show all these qualities too, but you must start believing in yourself. That is exactly what this book will help you learn to do.

You can shine your light in your corner of the world

and bring that light to other people when you let go of fear and keep learning lessons. When you believe in yourself, you can accomplish anything. You are an Amazing girl

Story of Colors

Do you sometimes want to play something, but others don't? Do you feel annoyed because they don't play what you do? It would be good for you to learn to try new things and open your mind to see what's out there.

Johanna was at school with her best friend, Mathew. It was a strange day since it was freezing and it rained all night. People didn't seem to want to leave the house, and the two had barely gone to their classroom.

The teacher was quiet and was leaving them to their own devices. Let them play and have as much fun as they wanted. For Johanna, it was a perfect day. They would have no homework, just play. She was 7 years old, just like her friend Mathew, the teacher was talking with other teachers, so Mathew and Johanna played.

They chased each other around the desks, took out the wooden cubes and made towers to see who would fall first, and played all sorts of games.

Johanna saw her friend amused at her things, playing with her and having a lot of fun while inviting her along. They made a stroller track with the box of cars they had in the living room.

They played to see who could tie the giant shoe first, which the teacher was teaching everyone to do.

They combed dolls, although Johanna didn't like them very much, as the school dolls were already manicured and looked like a witch with shaggy hair that would never be straight again, as surely many girls had tousled them.

Each of the games they chose lasted barely a while, as Mathew soon got bored, and they had to find something else. Johanna remembered that this was something she didn't like about her friend, because he seemed to get tired of everything, although she didn't realize it was the same, because if he played hide and seek, he soon got bored and wanted to do something else, if they played chase, he also got tired and wanted to play sitting down.

-Let's play that ghosts are going to invade us at school, said Johanna.

Mathew jumped for joy. He loved and was terrified of scary stories, he felt something in his stomach, but he always wanted to do it.

Then they started to play and took turns.

Then they moved the desks a little, and the teacher, who was entertaining the other teacher, looked at the two children.

-Everything all right over there? -she asked.

-Yes, teacher, everything is perfect. -Johanna said.

-What you messed up, you know you have to put it back in its place.

-Yes, teacher, said Johanna.

Johanna rolled her eyes, sighed, and kept looking for options.

-Let's have a race with electric robots?

Mathew seemed to get excited for a moment, but then he thought about it and decided against it.

-You're giving me a hard time, let's see... shall we play spies with the magnifying glass, looking for clues?

-Bored.

-Let's play that I'm a YouTuber, and you watch me.

-It's more boring.

-Shall we color the book?

-Not today, not ever.

-You're insufferable. -What do you want to play?

-What else is there?

-There are few options left.

Johanna was beginning to lose her patience. Every time Mathew said "boring," she got angrier and angrier because he couldn't make up his mind about anything.

She wanted to keep calm as her mother taught her. She told her that she had to be emotionally intelligent, and she explained to her that it was about learning to control her emotions and to think twice before bursting at the first feeling she had. Johanna tried, but it was difficult.

-Let's get the ball out and play. -Johanna proposed.

-What laziness.

Johanna lost what little patience she had left.

-Well, let's find something to do; I'm tired of you.

Johanna was very upset, so she went to a desk, the one that was the farthest back in the room, and sat down with her arms crossed. She wanted to play, but she had lost her patience. In the position she was in, she had her back to her friend; at this moment, she didn't even want to see him.

Now she was the one who felt bored because she wanted to play, to have fun until the time they came to pick her up. At the beginning of the morning, she imagined that this would be a perfect day; she and her friend were alone to entertain themselves all morning with all the toys.

She closed her eyes and thought about what her mother had taught her to go to happy places when she felt that emotions made her lose control, so she started thinking about the amusement park, eating cotton candy, going for a walk with her mother, or with her little brother that she loved very much, although, like Mathew, he made her lose her patience sometimes.

She heard behind her back that Mathew seemed to be uncovering things, jars. She heard the sound of paper moving, and she heard something tearing the paper, sticky tape that was open. There was a whole development behind her.

But she still felt discomfort and refused to turn around to see what was going on.

Finally, she began to look out of the corner of her eye, and she saw Mathew in his own world, busy doing something. He had taken out some paper, had some paint, and was beginning to scribble things.

Finally, she saw him completely; he was amusing himself by drawing things with paint on paper and was beginning to put it on the wall where the teacher had authorized them to place what they were painting. He was carefully placing sheets of paper in order after he painted.

-I see you found what to do. - Johanna said to him.

Mathew looked at her and nodded.

-Can I play with you?

Mathew nodded. Then she got up and stood next to him, took a blank sheet of paper, and began to paint the first thing that came to her mind.

Soon she saw that Mathew was not doing something random. He was creating a story on the wall. The first image seemed to be that of a Santa's sleigh that was on a white background. It was at the North Pole, and in the next image, it was filling up with presents.

Little by little, the images told the story as the child painted it.

Johanna began to paint, following Mathew's story, they built in straight line sheets where Santa was preparing the sleigh and was putting the gifts house by house. Of course, each one made a drawing of what he wanted in his home, and so they filled the entire wall.

Johanna and Mathew had no problem finding what to play from that day on because something she learned is that you can let the others also think and choose or let go for a moment because the idea will come up, and not everything has to be with a stopwatch.

Sometimes the best experiences arise spontaneously. You don't have to have a plan to do everything. You never know what you might miss if you get carried away. Participating in new things can open you up to unimaginable worlds.

Two Languages

Are you afraid of what people will say about your culture? Do you think you are not part of a group even if you haven't shown what makes you stand out? This story shows how the world is full of cultures and can open you up to meeting more people.

Arya was getting ready to go to class. She was nervous and felt like she had butterflies in her stomach. It wasn't new what she was feeling, but it bothered her a lot. Every day at home, she felt comfortable, but when she left, it gave her a feeling of sadness, as if she was leaving something of herself behind. In a way, it was like that.

She spoke two languages, English and Hindi, by inheritance from her father, who was from India.

She knew that her classmates did not understand her language at school, so when she was with them, she felt she could not be herself.

-Alavida- said by way of farewell as she was leaving the house. She was saying goodbye to her mother and grandmother. Then, she walked out and down the driveway.

Once at school, after chatting with some friends, she waited for her class to start.

-Hi, Arya - said Matilda, her best friend. She sat next to her in the classroom.

Arya smiled softly at her and said,

-Hi.

Arya liked Matilda. She was a sweet and kind girl. She had short shoulder-length dark black hair, very different from hers, which was thicker and a little longer.

Matilda liked to sit next to Arya, as they talked a lot, and in the off hours, they would play games or talk about anything. This was something Arya always appreciated.

At the beginning of class, Arya settled into her seat and watched the others answer various questions they were asking about the subjects. Although she knew the answers to almost everything, she didn't feel comfortable participating.

When the teacher finished the lineup of questions, she handed out a test. Arya saw that it was something about math. She knew quite a bit about the subject, but she felt nervous, anxiety began to quicken her breathing, and she began to feel a little choked up.

Arya took out the pencil case, and because she was so anxious, when she tried to open it, it slipped out of her hands and fell to the floor. The pencils began to roll like little cylinders lying down, and the crash of the wood on the floor made the whole room look at her.

Every one of her classmates turned to look at her, and Arya felt her face burning. She looked down and whispered:

-Mujhe Maaf Karen (I'm sorry).

She started to pick everything up quickly and felt someone tap her on the shoulder. She turned and saw:

-Shall I help you?

It was her friend who wanted to help her.

-Yes, you are very kind, she said.

They quickly picked up the things and put them in the pencil case and the bag.

-What was that you said when you dropped your things? -she asked her later.

Arya did a little memory recall and said she had felt it. Then she felt sorry, she hadn't thought that others had heard her, and then she said:

-My father is from India, and we have a lot of his culture; we speak Hindi at home. It's something I say when I feel a little sorry. I say sorry to apologize.

-That's great, said Matilda.

The teacher announced that they were now back to the test. They had already picked up all the mess.

-I'm sorry, teacher, said both girls. They finished putting things away and sat down in their seats.

-I want to know more about that language you speak, said Matilda.

-We talked about it at lunch.

Arya felt pride and surprise. She didn't think other people, not even Matilda, would be interested in knowing about her culture.

When they finished eating, both friends sat down on a bench in the small school playground, and Arya looked to the side. Almost the whole room was watching her.

A boy who had never spoken to her before said to her a little shyly:

-Matilda said that you could tell us about your other language, that thing you said in class.

Arya looked at her friend, winked, and gave him a thumbs up, amused.

-I think it's great that you're speaking more languages. -said another boy.

-Several of them are interested in learning more about you since they have never met anyone who speaks other languages.

They all seemed excited to meet her.

Arya was surprised that so many people wanted to know more about her language and that she could tell them anecdotes or whatever. They all looked at her with curiosity and in a friendly manner. She realized that she had practically never spoken to them before.

Now she felt a little embarrassed, and she blushed, for it was not comfortable to be the center of attention. Matilda stood next to her and smiled at her to encourage her. She said to her:

-You don't have to; it's not obligatory. But I think you are special and everyone wants to know more.

Arya thought about it some more, sighed deeply, and then said, Okay:

-Okay. What do they want to know?

So, each child began to speak at a time, and she asked them one at a time, then they began:

-Water.

-Paanee

-Sweets

-Meetha

-Cold

-Sardee.

So, one by one, they asked her words that she answered. At the end, a girl asked her:

-How is it that you speak two languages and especially that rare language?

-My family came to this country years ago, specifically my dad, and at home, we grew up with Indian culture. They helped me learn English and Hindi. I even speak a little Spanish.

Everyone was shocked that she spoke all those languages.

-How many languages are there in the world? -asked one child.

Another boy, who was very astonished and apparently from another classroom, looked at her and asked her many questions.

Arya thought the question was a very good one. She had never stopped to think about how many languages there were in the world. She saw Matilda, and she was smiling very sweetly. Maybe she had always known that Arya wasn't happy without showing some of who she was. Her culture, her language. It was no longer a secret, and the heartfelt more relieved to be rid of that weight.

Arya set about explaining to everyone what things meant, how it was part of the culture, and that the letters were not the same as the alphabet they knew but others that would surely look like scribbles to her.

She wrote some things down for them, and everyone was surprised that they now had more questions. Arya felt very comfortable chatting with her friends and showing the Hindu part of her life. She was grateful to Matilda for helping her take that step she had held back so much before. Arya approached her friend, hugged her, and said shukriya.

-What does that mean?

-Thank you. You are a great friend.

-You are too, and I love sharing with you.

-And me.

-Will you teach me how to speak Hindi?

-Of course, you have to work hard because it's a complex language.

-I'm sure if you teach it to me, it won't be so hard.

Arya already knew that many people appreciated her for who she was and how she showed her way of being. She felt happier.

She wanted to go home and tell her family what she had experienced that day. It was wonderful to speak two languages.

You have to be comfortable with who you are, learn to be yourself, and love yourself fully. Try to see beyond what people believe and expect of you. You may be surprised to discover that you were wrong about what others thought. You may enter a wonderful world full of great experiences where you will grow and learn new things.

Learn to embrace your culture and don't be afraid or ashamed to show it to the world; the world is full of many cultures and ways of being.

Respecting The Rules

Have you ever gone to other houses and been given rules that you don't understand why they exist? Do you feel like breaking the rule you are being asked to follow? This story is about how a little girl understood that an uncle was right to ask her not to do something.

Mia's relationship with her uncle was strange because she saw him from time to time. He had excellent humor, they played, and he always told some very funny joke that made her laugh. He also had a side of the character. He said that he liked people to do things correctly to comply with the rules because that was how the world could function correctly.

Mia was a 9-year-old girl, lovely, with long hair that reached her waist and that she took care of carefully every day. She was also a big fan of animals, especially dogs. She liked cats, but not so much.

One of the reasons why she liked to go to her uncle's place was because he had a dog named Olaf, a very playful German shepherd with whom she got along very well. They played, they chased each other, and he licked her until, in the end, she felt that all her skin smelled like dog, but she did not mind because she loved him very much.

Although her uncle was severe with the orders to the dog, they could only play in certain areas of the house, he could not take her to others, and they had time for play. He said:

-Dogs that are left too long on soft things like playing turn into kittens, and I want a dog to take care of.

The uncle worked as a mechanic, and in the evenings, he would leave the dog inside the garage, next to the house, guarding it in case someone wanted to get in, the German shepherd would bark at him, and he wouldn't dare.

The uncle had the idea that if Olaf played too much, one night, instead of protecting the workshop, he would open it so that whoever wanted to enter would be able to get in comfortably and look for what he wanted to take.

The trips to his uncle's place happened from time to time. They lived in the same city but from one end to the other. Mia's mother, her uncle's sister, was the one who took her every two weeks or once a month to visit and stay for a day.

-Niece! -said the uncle with joy, let's see which fish wears a tie.

-I don't know, said Mia after thinking about it for a while and giving up.

-The neck!

Everyone laughed because he always had a bad joke to tell.

That day of the visit, besides having Olaf in the back of the house, there was in the living room, on one of the furniture, an orange cat, asleep with its paws stretched out and deep.

-This one is as he wants to be, - said Mia's mother to her daughter.

-What a comfort this cat is, lazy, - said Mia.

-It's Luciano, - said the uncle -he's been here for a few days.

-He's cute. Can I play with Olaf? -said Mia.

-Yes, but on one condition.

-Okay.

-You can't bring him in the house for anything.

-But this is where we always play.

-This time, it can't be because these two don't get along. They play in the workshop.

After the siblings ate, Mia's mother left and said she would be back in a few hours and that she would stay with her uncle. She asked her to behave well and to comply with the rules.

Mia resigned and went to the workshop. There was a big and badly parked truck, leaving a small space to play. When Olaf felt her friend nearby, she looked for play, and they chased each other several times around the truck.

Mia hit the bumper three times, and in some parts, she had to pass sideways because of the wall or the tool machine.

-My uncle didn't know how to park this, she said, it's ugly to play like that.

Mia looked inside the house, but her uncle was not around. She saw Olaf and snapped her fingers to be followed. The dog did not move. What he did was tilt his head with a questioning expression.

Mia looked at him again and said:

-Come, I permit you.

The dog, still hesitating, followed her, sniffing everything, feeling that he was not on his ground. When they reached the living room, the place where they usually played on previous trips, the dog stopped and put on an expression of anger.

Luciano, the cat, stood up, and all his hair stood on end.

Instantly the dog went after the cat, and the cat went after him in a fit. The two began to chase each other, taking whatever they could find with them.

Ornaments fell to the floor, a small library with books fell, a car door was on one side, and it turned and hit the floor, and in less than a minute, the whole house was upside down.

Mia chased the dog, trying to stop it and also the cat but had no luck.

-What's going on here? -said the guy who appeared screaming. He took three steps and grabbed Olaf by the leash, dragging him while he shouted furiously at the cat, who was watching him angrily from afar.

The uncle left the dog in the workshop and locked him up. Now his cold gaze fell on Mia.

-Remember I asked you not to let the dog in?

Mia nodded ruefully.

-What was going to happen?

-They were going to fight with the cat.

-That's right, you see what happened.

The uncle turned his back on her and went to the backyard, then came back with a broom, a mop, a bucket, and disinfectants.

-Do you see how wet the floor is?

-Yes.

-The cat or the dog peed while fighting. You're going to clean it up and pick it up.

What took the dog and cat less than a minute to destroy took Mia two hours to pick up, tidy up, mop the floor, and clean thoroughly, she was sorry that her uncle was upset.

When she finished, the house was sparkling clean and didn't seem to have had room for a dog and cat fight.

The fear Mia had was that when her mother arrived, the uncle would accuse her, but she didn't. Maybe the lesson of having to clean the whole floor and tidy every corner without anyone's help had been enough.

She learned that she should not break the rules in someone else's house and that she had to be attentive to what her elders told her. If she was in someone else's house and they gave her an order not to touch or move the pet, even if it bothered her because she could not play well, she had to obey it because there was a reason for it.

The next time she went to her uncle's house, there were no cars, and she was able to play with Olaf all over the workshop, but she had to make sure she met the cat.

Sometimes there are rules that we don't like, but we are in someone else's house, or an adult asks us to do it, and we must respect it. They have their reason for asking you not to do something. If you want to do it, ask permission first.

Life in The Garden

Have you ever found birds' nests or ants' houses in your house? Do you know that this is their world? They live there every day, and you must protect their home? This is a story where a little girl discovers some animals in her house in a very bad place for her, but that makes her recognize the value she has.

Chloe was a very funny little girl. She loved to play and made friends very easily. When she arrived at the park, soon after, she had three or four children with her, and they would go to play in a group. She was the most popular at school and loved to play and have fun.

Something she loved was the parks. Every time one of her parents had some time, he took her to one that was close to home. She would ride, jump on the slide, swing, and play with each one of the attractions, the one that went around the climbing one, and hide and seek with other children. She would stay there until her parents asked her to come home, and she would leave, missing the park.

One day, her parents were talking in the bedroom. They thought that an ideal birthday present for Chloe would be to set up a park in the back part of the house, where they had a garden, a grill to barbecue on special occasions, and some dishes they never used, where she could have as much fun as she wanted and even invite her friends.

So, her parents began to build the park. However, first, they had to clean, remove weeds, eliminate useless elements, and leave the whole area clear. When Chloe asked what was going on, she was told they wanted to clean it up so it would look nice. Then, her father joked that he would put in a small soccer field to play with her friends.

While Chloe was at school, they installed one of those plastic and metal playgrounds that could be set up in a few hours, just a day before her birthday. So, when she came home from school, she found the best surprise, her playground had been installed, she could play at home as much as she wanted and it was the best birthday present she could have received.

-Can I use it now? -asked

-Yes. Even though your birthday is tomorrow, you can go now, said her father.

The little girl ran out and was about to climb on the swing when she ran into something she didn't expect.

-Dad! Come and see this.

The father, in a hurry, looked out, expecting to see some dangerous animal or that the playground had a loose piece since they had installed it in a hurry before she arrived.

But no, what was there was a small nest, a doe, and three tiny bunnies.

-It's a nest with some bunnies, said Chloe.

-Yes, and they just settled here, or we didn't see them, because when we were setting everything up, that hole wasn't there.

-Now I won't be able to play in my playground, said the little girl to herself.

-Well, it's his environment, shouldn't you? She has those bunnies there, and she takes care of them.

-Why does he seem to look at us with anger? -Chloe asked.

-It's not anger. She's just scared, and at the same time, she's looking at us defensively because she doesn't want us to hurt her. She's a mother protecting her children.

-Ya.

-Do you remember when we went to grandma's house?

Chloe remembered that her grandmother lived on a farm on the outskirts of the city, where there was a whole series of animals, pigs, cows, and even an old horse. In the back, there was a corral and chickens. When she looked out to see them, they had chicks, she bent down to take one, and she didn't know where from. A hen came out and chased her and gave her a series of pecks. She never imagined that a hen could peck so hard.

At that time, her mother told her that she could not take the hen's offspring without her permission because she was defending them. She had intruded into her space, which is why she had reacted that way.

Although at that time Chloe was very angry with the hen and spent the rest of the walk looking with annoyance at that coop, now that she had those bunnies in her territory, she saw with regret how her shiny, new-smelling park was waiting for her to play, but starting to do so endangered the bunnies.

It was a mixed feeling that overwhelmed her. She didn't know how to react.

-I know how much you love to play in the park, and having one in your backyard makes a dream come true.

-Yes, - Chloe interrupted him, - but right now, there are the rabbits, but I want to play.

-In life, we find ourselves in situations like that, where we have something very nice to enjoy. Still, we can't at that moment because something gets in the way, and we have to think about what is better.

-I want to play...

-You have your park, one of your birthday presents, you choose what is best. I think you already have the idea and answer in your little head.

Chloe was left alone, looking at the bunnies and the rabbit that kept looking at her. Finally, she got up, frustrated and annoyed with the rabbits, and went inside. This time she spent the rest of the day without looking at the backyard because, from any of the windows, the bright colors of the whole park were projected, making her sadder.

That night the parents talked about how the girl would have to wait to be able to play in her park. They even questioned why they didn't notice when they installed it or when the rabbit appeared with her young. Still, nothing could be done. Animals were often wiser than humans.

The next day, Chloe's birthday, she got up very early and silently went out to the backyard with some things in her hand. She didn't want anyone to realize what she was going to do. Quietly she prepared her plan. She would not let anything ruin her enjoyment of her park.

When her parents got up, they went to the bedroom and didn't find her. She was finishing setting everything up when they went to the backyard. She stood up like a spring and saw her parents in surprise.

-Happy birthday to me, and happy birthday to the bunnies, she said.

-What did you do? -asked the mother.

-I put up the little house for them.

-You didn't bother them, did you? -said the father.

-No, I didn't even peek. I just did this.

There was a big sign made with crayons and cardboard and decorated with lots of little things I had, and it said "Welcome Home and Happy Birthday."

Chloe learned that animals choose to nest in any place because they see it as suitable and safe for their offspring, the doe had chosen that nest for a reason, and she had to respect it.

She enjoyed her part while the rabbits were growing, and then when they were out and safe, she could now fully enjoy her park.

Humans occupy space, but it is not only ours. Other species also inhabit it. Therefore, we must respect their habitat and not remove them, even if they are on our property.

The New Hamster

Do you want a pet, and do your parents talk to you about the responsibility it implies? In this story, you will meet Sabrina, a little girl who had a great experience with her first pet.

Sabrina had always wanted to have a pet. All her classmates had one. Many had cats, others had dogs, and one had a bird or fish. However, she was the only one who did not have a pet yet.

She had asked her parents, and they told her that she would have to have several responsibilities if she wanted to have a pet. They were not sure if she was ready to assume them.

Sabrina said yes, that she would not fail in anything and would take care of everything the pet would need.

After a family consensus, her parents decided that this first pet would be a hamster, which would be in a special house, with the food and the elementary care it implied.

The day they announced to Sabrina that they would go to the pet store to get the hamster, she was a little upset because although she wanted a pet, she was unsure if it would be the ideal one. Still, they told her that the care was simple and she would prove that she was responsible enough to have a bigger one in the future.

Although when she got to the store and saw all the cages full of animals, she walked up to the hamster and saw them. They looked like cute little balls of fur to her.

-Is this your first pet? -asked the owner of the store who approached.

-Yes, said the mother, she will have her first pet. Let's see how she behaves in her care.

-Well, this is an excellent pet, you'll see!

The lady saw Sabrina, who had a confused face as if she wasn't sure if she wanted a hamster.

-Come, she said as she opened the cage a little; go on, reach in, and carefully touch the one you want.

Sabrina reached into the cage, touched one that was brown with white, and saw her from the beginning. As soon as she got close, she felt its softness, delicacy, and how it carefully climbed into her hand and began to move. She laughed because it tickled.

It was love at first sight.

-I think you have chosen your new friend.

The lady put the hamster in a little box that she tied tightly with little holes on the sides so it could breathe. Sabrina carried her new friend in her hands, careful not to let the box move too much, as if she were carrying a bowl full of soup.

When they arrived home, they set up the new cage and placed the floor, water, food, and everything they needed.

-This is the place where your pet has to be, said the mother as she showed him how to put the hamster in the cage. After you put it in, you have to close it, make sure it fits snugly, and then put the latch on like this.

He placed a hook that went into a hole and closed perfectly.

-You have to make sure it closes well so it won't escape because they are curious and always seem to be electric, always looking for something to do, with mischief at the doors of their little heads.

-Yes, Mommy, I'll keep an eye on them.

The mother left Sabrina alone with the pet; now that they were both seeing each other, she said to him:

-I have a dilemma, and it is that I still don't know what I am going to call you. So many names have gone through my mind, but I don't know if you like them.

The hamster looked at her with his little red eyes shining and wiggling his little mouth.

-What do you think of the name Maurice? You look like you have that name.

The hamster walked over and brushed her hand, seeming to tell her he liked the name.

-Maurice will be your name.

From that day on, the two of them played. Sabrina watched some videos on the internet, and with cardboard, school glue, and tape, she made him a tunnel where she put him in. He ran all over the place from one side to the other. She put little treats in the food he was looking for. Even though he was a small pet, there seemed to be communication between them.

-Remember to clean the floor of Maurice's cage, her parents warned her, remembering part of the responsibilities involved.

-Yes, Mom.

-While you were at school, I gave him water, and he immediately started drinking it. How long has it been since you gave him water? -His father said.

It was about two days since I had put it on him, and she regretted that she had forgotten to put it on.

One day, when she came home from school, her parents looked at her with a worried air, as if they had been dreading that moment.

-What's wrong? -Sabrina asked.

-It's Maurice.

-What's wrong with him?

-He's not here. -Said the father.

-Did you close him well? -asked the mother.

Sabrina thought at the time that she had locked him up, and she could have sworn that she had, but the cage was open, so it surely was not.

Sabrina spent the rest of the day looking in every corner of the house, walking as if she were stepping on eggs to avoid accidentally stepping on them and killing them. She looked in every space, her toys, under the bed, between the pillowcases, in the boxes, everywhere, but he seemed to have been swallowed by the earth.

The more she searched in every corner without luck, the sadder Sabrina felt, for her first pet seemed to have vanished.

-Is he all right?

-Maybe he went out of a window, daughter, those little animals are very intelligent and agile. I hope he got to another house and, that he was adopted, that he is well.

-I miss him a lot.

-I know, daughter, you should have been more careful with his door and the other things in his care.

Sabrina said nothing but felt sad; she was sorry that Maurice was gone.

The days passed, and there was no more trace of the hamster. When they thought he was lost, the mother picked up the cage and put it in the storage room, and the food container was put in the pantry to donate later to someone with a hamster.

One day, when Sabrina least expected it, she got up. It was a Saturday. She went to her bathroom and opened the door of a small cabinet where she had her toothbrush and toothpaste. As she did so, a pair of little eyes looked at her carefully; it was Maurice!

Tremendous was her joy to find that her pet had been around the house or had gone out, but he had been lucky enough to come back and be there, waiting for her. Everyone at home was very happy, they took the cage out again, and the lesson helped Sabrina to start taking more care of her pet from that day on.

From that day on, she always cleaned the cage, put food and water in it, and when she closed it, she confirmed twice that it was locked. When she went to school, she placed the side of the cage door towards the wall to avoid any mischief from Maurice.

Having pets is very nice, but they have responsibilities. Besides proof of love for them, it is also for their welfare; you can put them in danger if you don't take care of them as they deserve.

Where is The Jewelry?

When you do something wrong with a friend or family member, do you take responsibility? Do you know the importance of facing the consequences of your actions? This is a story where a fun game between sisters teaches a great lesson.

Hanna and Lisa were two sisters who were a year apart from each other. Both had the good fortune to grow up in loving homes with parents who loved each other very much and whose only mission was to take care of them. They were always intensely dedicated to making sure that they lacked nothing and that they were happy children.

As in every home, there were many traditions, like ordering pizza on Thursdays, Hanna liked the one with ham and cheese, and Lisa liked the one with pineapple, so they would order one of those that was half and half so that everyone would be happy.

On Saturdays, they would go out to the mall to play in one of the parks, and there were also traditions of responsibilities, such as brushing their teeth when they got up, flossing twice a day, and giving thanks before going to sleep for all the good and bad things that happened during the day.

Among the traditions that existed in the family was that at the end of every month, when the father received his month's salary, he would bring a little gift to each of them, it was not as incredible as a birthday present or those brought by Santa, but it was something that both girls had in their plans to acquire, either because their classmates had it at school or because they saw it in a family outing to the supermarket or on an errand.

So, during the month, there was always a plan:

-Daddy, - Hanna would say, -I know what I want you to bring me when you get paid, a rag doll we saw at the supermarket...

-And I want the Rubik's cube I saw in... - said Lisa.

-All right, girls. Count on it. But it comes at a price.

They both knew what it was all about and began to chase them around the house to end up in a tickle ration or caught by the "monster."

As usual, some toys become fashionable for a while. Every child has one. One that both Hanna and Lisa were dazzled by was a beautiful trunk filled with many golden designs and purple as the main color. It had a door that opened with a combination and where the owner could put any key she wanted.

Both Hanna and Lisa dreamed of having it. It was seen in all the toy store windows, it was reviewed on social networks, and everyone wanted one, so the girls' parents were not surprised when they asked for it.

- I'll see what it costs. If it's not expensive and it fits in the budget of the monthly detail, count on it. -Said the father.

Indeed, the price was affordable, it was made of plastic, but it was strong enough to hold a lot of things inside.

- When I have it with me, I will fill it with many things. I will put the dolls in it, I will put Bear in it, and I will store food. -said Hanna, who was the youngest.

- You can't put Bear in it because it's too big, and you can't put food in it either. It will get damaged. -said, Lisa.

- Well, but I'll put more things in, you'll see.

They both waited anxiously for daddy's payday to arrive so that he would show up at home that afternoon with the presents, but the more you wait for something, the slower the calendar seems to get.

Finally, dad got paid, that day was the longest of all, and he usually showed up at 7 pm. That day, for some reason, he arrived at 7:10 pm, and it was the longest 10 minutes for them.

When he walked through the door, Lisa jumped:

- Where were you?

The father was surprised by the greeting, and Lisa immediately corrected him:

-Hello, daddy. Sorry, we are excited.

The father smiled and said:

-Well, there was a long line at the store where I bought some things.

-What things? -said Hanna, already suspecting what it was about.

-Well... -she reached into a big bag and took out two things- This!

Finally wrapped were the two boxes. They were a cube wrapped in pink paper of dolls and bears. She handed one to each of them, and they both dropped to the floor to tear the paper. Immediately a purple box with a design similar to the toy appeared, they opened it, and finally, each had their safe to play with.

They saw the instructions and put a password on it that only each one knew.

-What password did you put on it? -Hanna asked.

-We don't say... It's a secret! What password did you give?

-I won't tell either... It's a secret!

After setting them up, what followed was figuring out what to put inside the box. They both started playing with how they would store and protect the different things, mostly small toys, plastic rings, necklaces, and so on.

Lisa thought of a plan that she liked:

-What if we put mom's jewelry in?

Hanna's face lit up. She loved the idea.

Indeed, that safe was perfect for storing things.

In the meantime, mom and dad were downstairs, talking in the kitchen. Both girls went to their parents' room, opened the jewelry box, and divided all the jewelry between them. It was a small fortune that the family owned in precious materials. They had it both for special occasions and to have gold money.

They went to their room to play. There they lost themselves in their imagination, devising many scenarios with the jewels, making parades, and keeping them safe. They came out of their fantasies when dad appeared down the stairs and shouted in fright to the second floor.

-Love, we've been robbed.

The mother rushed upstairs and asked:

-What happened?

-They took the jewelry. Did you hear anything?

Both parents began to search the whole house for traces of theft, looking to see what else the supposed thief had taken.

Meanwhile, the frightened girls looked at each other, not knowing what to do, confessing that it had been them.Soon after, the father entered the room and saw them both on their knees on the floor, with the boxes open and all the jewelry inside. His face seemed to soothe immediately.

-Love, the girls have the jewels. They took them to play with, then, turning to them, don't they remember not to take the jewels?

-It was Lisa's idea, said Hanna, crying.

-Whoever's idea it was, they both participated. Besides, if you're involved, you can't turn your sister in at the first observation.

-They have two lessons to learn, first, remember that you don't play with mother's jewelry. They have plenty of toys, and second, Hanna, if they committed a prank, take responsibility, don't blame your sister right away, she may or may not have come up with the plan, but you participated, and you are just as guilty as she is.

Hanna felt bad and then offered apologies to her sister, and both promised not to take the jewelry again without permission

The two girls knew that by taking what they shouldn't, they could cause a big scare for their parents, plus if you don't take responsibility, there are consequences.

Take responsibility for your actions. In life you will make many mistakes, it is part of your growth, take responsibility for them, and do not blame others.

One for All and All for One

Have you ever been in a situation where everyone is looking for the same fate? Have you ever been punished for no fault of your own? This is a story that shows how friendship and loyalty help to keep you together with others.

Julia was a very sweet girl. She always behaved at school, did her homework and obeyed the teacher in everything she told them. She was one of the few who did things right in her classroom, as her classmates were very naughty. Although she was amused, she preferred to stay out of it because, at home, she had been taught to be well-behaved and not to bother the teacher.

-You must follow the rules, her mother always told her. So, when all the other children were running around the room, she stayed quiet.

The most she could do was to start coloring. She would take out a notebook with drawings and her crayons and start drawing, a friend would come and talk, and they would hang out, but always in her seat.

When her classmates misbehaved, the teacher would come out. Although in the last few days, they were more mischievous than ever, for some organizational reason at the school, the teachers would go to meetings at any time of the day, whenever the principal called them. This resulted in a jungle in every classroom where the children were having fun.

-Children, said the teacher before taking some things from her desk and leaving, we have to go to a meeting for a moment. Please be quiet, take notes on the board, and don't shout or jump on the seats.

All the children nodded, but about 10 seconds had passed since she had left the room when they all shouted in jubilation and started jumping up and down.

Some walked around the desks, stepping on one and another. Some took the backpacks of their classmates and turned them upside down, and emptied them.

If there was a fight pending between them, they would start playing and fighting. The girls usually sat around talking; groups were formed.

Next to Julia, there would be one or two and sometimes none. She was usually a loner, and she liked it. Deep down, she was glad that the teacher went out for a while, for she had a chance to start drawing her things.

Although the children did not go unpunished when the teacher returned as she said with annoyance that she had listened to them all the time, even though the meeting was barely heard over everyone's shouting. She told them to behave, or they would pay dearly for it.

At the beginning of the school year, an important event was prepared for the school, the anniversary week, a day when they celebrated the birthday of the school, a day when they did not do school activities but went to the fields or common areas to play, watch plays, enjoy the music or the food that different parents sold.

It was a very fun event for the children, eagerly awaited.

The meetings that the teachers were having with the director every day at all hours, it seemed, were to fine-tune last-minute details and vital information for the parents and children.

In one of those meetings where the children did everything, even turned over some desks, the teacher saw the mess when she returned and was annoyed:

-I see that you don't want to listen to me, children. I'm going to teach you all a hard lesson. Who knocked over those desks?

Nobody spoke. Not even Julia, who had done nothing. The teacher even asked her directly, but she kept silent.

-I'm going to tell them something. If they continue like this, I'm going to punish them with something that will surely serve as a lesson forever.

The children seemed to turn a deaf ear to her warnings because as soon as the teacher left the room, they started running around and looked more mischievous every day.

Julia thought about why this year her classmates had been so naughty, like electricians. Her mother told her that it could be because of the party atmosphere that was already in the school, and the events of the anniversary week, so they felt that Christmas-like air where they just wanted to play.

-Yes, Mom, but they are worse than ever.

-You behave well, as I have always taught you, her mother said and kissed her on the forehead. Julia nodded. She knew she had to behave.

On the day of the anniversary week, all the children were very excited because a magician was coming, some singers that they followed on social networks were coming, there would be an area to take pictures for the internet and many events. When they entered, they saw that all the courts were full of things to see, and this seemed to make them even more excited.

That day the teacher was more absent than usual, although she came now and then to the classroom to see the children, she had to go out, as they were preparing everything for the big event.

-Children, I have to go out a lot, please behave yourselves. Remember that I can punish you, don't make me take drastic measures.

As soon as I was out, the children started jumping all over the place, some of them thought it was funny to play earthquakes, and they started knocking down all the desks, and even Julia was lifted and had her seat knocked down.

She complained but to no avail.

When the teacher came in, she was wide-eyed.

-What happened here? -she said.

No one answered.

-Who did this?

No one said anything.

-Either you tell me who did it, or you're all grounded now.

Although some exchanged glances, no one said anything. Julia looked at the children, including those who had done the prank but said nothing. She wanted to open her mouth, to accuse them, but at the same time, she felt it was not the right thing to do.

-This is going to be the punishment. No one is going to the anniversary party. We're staying in the living room. I hope they like it and that they are the only ones who will miss it.

-Teacher, nooo! -Some said.

-They should have thought about it before doing this or telling me who did it. -She saw Julia and spoke to her- -Let's see, tell me, Julia, who was it?

-I didn't see. I was coloring.

The teacher saw her, knew she was a good girl, and said:

-I see that everyone behaved badly, except Julia, who I know is always in her seat, only she will go to the anniversary party, and the others will stay to solve divisions.

They all complained, and Julia felt uncomfortable. It is not what she wanted.

-No teacher, said Julia, I'm not going to the anniversary party. If we don't all go, I'm not going.

The teacher was surprised for a moment by what her student said.

-Well, I think that's a good deed you're doing. It's proof of a girl who is loyal to her group.

The teacher began to talk about Julia, she gave her as an example and then told them that they should behave better, that it was an effort of the whole school for this anniversary party.

The children who had committed the prank said with an embarrassed laugh that they had done that and that they were already picking everything up, they began to do it, and in a couple of minutes, everything was in order.

After a lengthy scolding, the teacher finally gave them all permission to go to the anniversary party.

Although Julia didn't commit mischief, she stayed loyal to her group and didn't give away or take preferences. It's part of teamwork.

Sometimes you have to be part of the team and not expect favoritism, as you are part of a group, and there should be equality for all.

Stop being invisible

Are you afraid to show who you are to the world? In the shelter of your home, do you do it without fear? Many girls struggle with shyness as they pursue their dreams. You may be afraid to pursue your goals. The story below will show you how you can become what you desire if you believe in yourself.

Abby had always been very shy, ever since she was a child. She had a hard time relating to others because she didn't know how to start a conversation. She even had a hard time participating in classes and got a lump in her throat when she had to answer questions.

But she had a special gift and that was that she could hide anywhere! If there was something her size or more people, she could hide so that no one would see her.

This sometimes came naturally to her, because she could not be seen even if she wanted to be seen at a certain moment. It was normal for her to be told:

-Abby, you're here, I hadn't seen you.

She didn't want to use invisibility, but it helped her when she needed it, especially when she was with other people, at school, or in the courses she was enrolled in. If someone called out to her, she could hide quickly so they wouldn't see her as easily. Then, when they weren't looking for her, she would go out and they wouldn't even notice. Although it was helpful to be like that, it could also be a problem, because she would get very nervous. It happened when there were a lot of people around and she didn't notice until someone called out to her.

One day when she was coming back from a swimming lesson, she realized that she had spent the whole day invisible, that no matter how close she was, no one saw her or talked to her, and no one determined her.

-I must be more careful, she said to herself.

One day when she was leaving school, she saw on the bulletin board a poster for a contest that attracted her very much. It would take place in less than a week and Abby wanted to take part since she had always been good at dancing and had taken some ballet classes. She had already practiced a modern mix that would serve to show a proposal that she was sure no one else had.

Once at home, she put on comfortable clothes and began to dance all afternoon, happy because she would achieve something.

She felt very confident.

That night she thought about the stage where she would perform, in front of hundreds of people watching her. She was so nervous that she froze. Even though she was alone, she felt she had to hide so as not to see herself in the reflection of the mirror.

-Okay, Abby, you have to do it. -She said to herself.

She started again in the mirror, she was more confident, but when she closed her eyes to start moving, she imagined herself in front of those people and even her mind made her think that they would boo her for her weird dance, for inventing what didn't exist.

She had no idea what she would do.

The day of the contest was near, so she didn't have much time to hesitate.

She thought that for now, she could devote herself to continuing to rehearse. The first thing was to remain visible, that is, not to hide from the others, but she was only partially successful. Shortly before the contest she hid again, it was a lot of pressure.

At school recess, she tried to talk to other people in the halls but felt it was too difficult, and after talking to a few acquaintances, she went and hid so as not to talk to anyone else. Anxiety was beginning to get the best of her, despite her fear of facing it.

With every minute that passed, the contest where she would dance was closer and she was ready to dance no matter the result.

On the day of the contest, her mother prepared her with a beautiful hairstyle, and a dress according to the occasion for the dance she had been working on and told her that she was surprised that she had signed up for those things, as she did not expect it from her, although she said she was glad she took those steps, as she deserved it because of how talented she was.

-I'm glad you're coming out of that shell you created.

Her mother smiled lovingly at her.

-Yes, but I'm scared, Mom. I'm nervous, I don't know if I'll do it right. I'd better not go to that.

That's for you to decide, daughter, but I still think you'll do great. If you want, I'll give you my secret to overcoming those nerves.

 Tell me.

-Close your eyes and take a deep breath, let the air fill your belly, and then breathe out, slowly, repeat several times and you'll see that little by little you'll start to feel serene.

-I don't think that will work for me, mom.

-If you don't try it, you won't know if it works or not.

-Thank you, Mom.

This conversation stayed with Abby and she thought about whether or not just breathing would help her. She wasn't sure about that remedy, nerves were playing tricks in her head and nothing was working. She was about to go on stage.

It was almost his turn and she began to see other children who were going to perform their talents in front of the others. Some were jumping with somersaults, others were singing, there was one who juggled with pine trees and there was one who even spits fire.

She noticed that they were all doing well and felt that maybe she could do little or worse, make mistakes, and be the mockery of everyone. She thought she could hide and dance, but realized it was hard to be seen. It didn't make sense.

-It's the turn of a dancer who is going to delight us with a new proposal, said the one who animated the contest, Let's give Abby a round of applause.

But Abby did not come out. The animator announced her again, although now a little worried.

Abby thought that she could run away, that no one would see her, it was easy really, and as she thought about it, the idea got into her head more solidly. But if she ran away, she wasn't going to face that fear and she wouldn't get used to the crowd anxiously waiting for her.

She remembered her mom's exercise and took a deep breath, took a step, and entered the stage. The entertainer seemed relieved and everyone applauded.

She slowly walked up with confident steps and everyone applauded her. This made her feel a little better. She got into the starting dance position and breathed again, controlling her fear.

She closed her eyes and started the dance, a few seconds later she had left aside that an audience was watching her with their mouths open, she was moving on the stage, and she had taken over the whole place. She felt lighter and lighter, the jumps seemed to lift her to the sky, and the movements seemed to move her quickly throughout the space.

When she finished, she took a few seconds, opened her eyes and her ears seemed to activate again, because everyone was clapping loudly and shouting happily.

She came in third place in the contest, but in the end, she didn't go for winning the contest, she went for participating, showing what she did and proving to herself that she could.

She returned home happy with her prize, third place for her was the biggest first place she had won so far, and all for not hiding from the world.

She wanted to prove to herself that she could dance in front of everyone. She had been seen and now many were imitating her dance as the coolest thing ever.

She promised herself that she would work to improve and that she would participate in other competitions, no matter how scared she was.

It's hard to deal with shyness, it takes time, especially it takes confidence, but when you believe in yourself, you can do anything you want.

The Giant Slide

How do you handle fear when it comes up? Do you try to tell it to go away, or do you let it take over? It's good to be cautious, but sometimes you can lose good things if you don't dare. This is a story where the adventure will lead you to learn that fear is good.

Lisa pedaled harder to give her bike more momentum and see how fast she could get to the corner. She knew she was going at high speed; she felt like she was going like a speeding car.

The sun was warming her skin, and she felt happy about that. Her cheeks and her whole skin were sweating, and this made her excited.

-Get in, Lisa! -Her father shouted to her from the house. She had already gone out to play a while ago.

Lisa went home, pedaling hard, and slowed down by kicking the back wheel a little.

She knew she couldn't do that everywhere, but in the driveway, she could because there was some dirt where she could brake. She was always looking to be sure before she did anything, even though she loved adventures.

Her father would tell her that there were ways to do things, the right and the wrong ways.

The amusement park had come to town, and on Saturday, they would go to visit, where they would spend the day riding all the rides with a single-pay handle where she could enjoy each place.

Early in the morning, they arrived to enjoy each attraction; there were many. She rode the up-and-down horses on the carousel, and although she was already bored, it was for younger children. She went to a park where she could climb obstacles and go down small slides or over rope obstacles without any danger.

She rode in the bumper cars and had fun until she got tired and almost hoarse from screaming while hitting other cars. When time ran out, she would line up again and try again.

She climbed into a boat that waved back and forth and felt her stomach contract with each movement, which made her laugh a lot.

Although since she had arrived, she was watching an attraction that intimidated her; it was a giant slide-like building, bright yellow, where everyone went. They would go up a bunch of stairs and then sit on a thick fabric that looked like a boat. The girl who worked there would push, and for a few seconds, the person would go down until they fell.

It looked fun but also challenging.

Apparently, because of this attraction, Lisa was more excited than usual. Her mother asked her to calm down, then she said:

-Mom, I've never seen anything like that slide; it's gigantic.

-It looks good, goes and jumps on it. Go and get in line.

Lisa ran off and got to the end. She stretched her neck and saw the face of each person that jumped, with fear and also with adrenaline and happiness for this adventure.

Now that she was close, she realized how high it was. The attraction looked like a tower.

She waited patiently for the slow passing of the line, looked around, and talked to the others who were waiting, and each one showed how exciting it was.

-Great.

-I can't wait to jump.

-It's my 20th time

-Long ago, I almost turned around and cracked my head open.

-You didn't hold on tight, said another.

-You have to hold on to the handles that the lady points out to you, said another.

-Yes, it only happened once, now I'm holding on tight, and it didn't happen again.

Fear began to dominate Lisa, but she said to herself:

-Goodbye fear, you have to leave me alone, this is not dangerous.

She felt the doubts and the fear overwhelming her, and this was consuming her little by little.

The anxiety seemed to weaken her legs, and she wanted to run away to be by her mother's side. The feeling was so great that she wanted to go to where her mother should be.

It was almost her turn, so she decided she'd better go to where her family was. Her mother would tell her something good, and she could be better off.

She saw the boy she had talked to earlier and said to him:

-I have to go get something I forgot. Please take care of my stall.

-Sure- the boy said.

She went until she found her mother and hugged her tightly to regain her confidence. She hugged her back.

-Are you all right, daughter?

-I'm afraid to get on it.

She trembled with fear and cried.

-I've never seen you so scared of anything. It must have been terrifying.

She nodded.

-What was so scary?

-It's loud, a kid said. He almost cracked his head open.

-The kid was in line?

-Yes.

-Then it must not have been so bad if he repeated.

She was still very anxious, and her mother asked her to take slow, deep breaths so that she would begin to calm down.

-You don't have to go upstairs and jump in if you don't want to.

Lisa bit her lip and became thoughtful.

-But I want to do it.

-If you want to do it, you have to overcome that fear then.

-I think so.

-You know, when you're afraid of something, it means you're worrying more about doing what you want to do. We all have fear when we try something new or when what we do is important. Fear is an alarm that tells you to be careful, but sometimes it becomes a bad thing. If you want to launch yourself out of that place, you have to embrace the fear. Those things are made with safety in mind, so I'm sure if you follow the instructions, nothing will happen to you.

Lisa looked at the attraction again and saw that it was almost her turn; the sense of adventure and the desire to take that jump made her almost run.

-Will you come with me? -She said to her mother.

-Of course, I'm coming with you. -Her mother told her.

They went hand in hand, and she accompanied her to the end of the line. When she was almost at the top, she noticed that he was not as tall as she had seen him before. She was holding her mother's hand and squeezing it. Before she knew it, it was her turn to jump.

Having her mother close by had given her the strength she needed to be able to take that step. Things didn't seem as scary now as they had before. Her chest tightened a little when it was going to touch him, but she spoke to the fear.

-Fear for what? -No reason to be afraid like that.

Fear kind of heard her because it went away.

That's when she realized that fear wasn't fear; it wasn't because she was going to throw herself off that big slide; she was good at it.

Lisa turned to look at her mom and said with her lips, "Thank you."

She grabbed the fabric as she was told, gripped the handles tightly, and let herself go, she screamed with joy as she went down, and the fear in her stomach wasn't so unpleasant.

She climbed out and stood at the end of the line again; it was just the beginning of great fun that was sure to end at the end of the day.

If you build your confidence, you can quiet that fear that wants to consume you; that's what Lisa did to overcome the fear of heights and the new.

When you let fear control you, you lose, but when you overcome it, you can live better. As long as you are safe, do what you want to do, no matter what fear tells you.

Hidden Talent

Have you ever seen a child at school and found him or her a little withdrawn or different? Have you discovered that this person has an incredible talent for something? This is a story that teaches you that you shouldn't judge by what a person shows because underneath can hide someone great.

Maggie was in third grade at her school. Since kindergarten, she had been in the same school, so she had the same classmates since they were almost babies. They knew each other since they pronounced slurred words and started to speak better. Some learned to say the "R" with no problem. Each one had lived a different story and a joint one, being classmates.

So, apparently, they knew each other perfectly. They knew that Peter was the most mischievous and loved to fight with his classmates and, at recess, play more roughly than the others. Every few weeks, the teacher would get angry and ask him to bring his mother to complain about his behavior. They knew that Mia was a math genius and had beautiful handwriting, they knew that Sophia was the most suitable for speeches because she did it perfectly, and they knew that Timothy, or Timo as they all called him, was the quietest and most withdrawn. For years he had been the butt of the other children's jokes.

As they all knew each other, they knew how to choose the one who was the best candidate for the job.

-Let's put on a play and I'll choose the actors. -Said the teacher. We'll do Romeo and Juliet, and there will be some singing scenes.

Maggie was thrilled by this, for she was good at singing, and whenever she could, she began to sing different lyrics.

-Maggie will undoubtedly be Juliet, as she is one of the great singers in this room.

Maggie felt excited; she knew what she was. She waited anxiously to see who would be her accompanist.

-And for the role of Romeo, I choose Timo.

All the children in the room made a sound that resembled a:

-What? -but they immediately fell silent.

Timo himself opened his eyes wide and looked at the teacher, thinking that he was facing something horrible from which no one would save him.

-It's a decision, said the teacher, Timo, I know you can do it.

Timo didn't even speak; he seemed to sink into his desk.

The rest of the class was spent choosing other characters and defining the idea with liberties that Shakespeare's play would have.

When Maggie arrived home, her mother was tidying up some things in the kitchen and looked at her worriedly.

-What happened to you, daughter? Why are you like this? Did they do something to you?

-They chose me to act in a play, and I'm going to sing, said Maggie with a sad look on her face.

-But that's incredible! It's what you've always wanted; congratulations, daughter.

-It will be Romeo and Juliet.

-Wow, I didn't expect that play. I'm sure the teacher will make her adjustments, and who are you?

-Juliet.

-The principal! Congratulations again. Why do you have that little face, then?

-Romeo is going to be Timo.

The mother froze for a moment as if analyzing the situation, then she said.

-Daughter, I imagine you think it's going to be a disaster with that child, but you shouldn't judge someone by what you see above.

-Mom, we've known each other since we were three years old, since we were babies, a lifetime.

The mother smiled.

-Daughter, I'm sure you will be surprised. Give him a chance. Besides, your teacher is very smart; she would have her reasons for choosing him.

Maggie spent the day thinking about it and how it might be a great idea. She thought her first big number would be a disaster.

She thought she had no choice but to go see her partner since the teacher had defined that Romeo and Juliet would practice every chance they got. They were given the lyrics and some audio to prepare. The rehearsals would begin later.

Timo had always been a shy boy. When he entered the school, Peter, who befriended him, soon saw that he was more fearful than the others and began to make jokes; this was enough for Timo to become shy and insecure and so for years, he had withdrawn, and everyone believed that he would not have the blood to stand before a stage.

But the teacher saw something that the others did not.

Resigned, Maggie arrived at Timo's house, knocked, and soon after, a very kind lady opened the door. It was her mother.

-Hello Maggie, Timo is waiting for you, he's in his room, go on.

Maggie had never been to Timo's house. It was very nice and tidy. They had a big library with hundreds or thousands of books and, in the back, a wall full of musical instruments, guitars, saxophones, and a piano in the center of the room.

As she approached the room his mother had pointed out to her, a melody she had heard in the distance became more noticeable and louder, she thought it was something put on the radio, but to her surprise, as she peeked through the door, there was Timo, with a pose that made him look taller and a voice that he didn't know where it came from that boomed off the walls.

-Timo!

The boy fell silent immediately and seemed to shrink twenty centimeters and saw Maggie with the same frightened expression as always.

-You sing... incredible.

-Thank you, he said after searching for the words.

-No one at school knows you sing like that; you're a born performer.

-I'm ashamed to do it.

-You shouldn't, and you look... I don't know how to explain it. Incredibly, incredible when you sing, you look like someone else.

-I don't just sing. I do more things; I'm just afraid they'll make fun of me at school for it.

-I don't think they will. They make fun of you because they think you don't know how to do anything, but you do. I even feel ashamed to sing.

-You sing very well too. I'm sure we'll do well.

That day they both began to see each other's lyrics and how the play was going. It didn't take them long to get in tune and sing, as well as if they had rehearsed for months. They made the perfect duo, he with a strong and incredible voice for a child and she with that soft melody.

When they rehearsed the play at school with the other actors, all the kids were preparing the jokes and had ideas of how Timo would ruin it. When they heard the voice and how it transformed, they were amazed. From that day on, they changed the way they saw their classmate and learned later that he had withdrawn from showing his essence because of how they had teased him for years.

The play was one of the best the school had ever seen. The parents gave a standing ovation, and Timo saw Maggie at the end and said "Thank you" with his lips.

She hadn't done much, though, just remind him of who he was.

Maggie also learned not to judge the first time. You can know someone for a long time and be surprised at how they have hidden talents you didn't know about.

You should never judge a person by how they show up at first, as Timo had a great talent, besides singing he was a voracious reader, he knew about many subjects, only fear ruled him, now he has loosened up and transformed at school. The jokes to classmates and thinking that the quiet or withdrawn do not know anything is not right. Never judge anyone. Behind every personality, there is a series of fact that have made him that personality.

Made in the USA
Las Vegas, NV
28 November 2023

81561127R00056